Challenge - Rise - Triumph

Mandy Robinson

Presentation by *BookLeaf Publishing*

Web: www.bookleafpub.com

E-mail: info@bookleafpub.com

ISBN: 9789357696999

First edition 2023

DEDICATION

For my daughter Sabrina and grandson David with love

And

To all who read this book, may you be inspired along your own journey to keep rising to greater heights and successes! I believe in you!

ACKNOWLEDGEMENT

Grateful thanks to Book Leaf Publishing.for
setting a great challenge to all poets to write 21
poems in 21 days!
I've really enjoyed stepping fully into, and
completing the challenge, with great joy!!

PREFACE

This book will make you pause, ponder and think deeply about your own life and how nature can teach us much about finding the lessons we need to learn to succeed and thrive.

Mandy E. Robinson is a bestselling author, editor, proofreader and legacy ghostwriter. Inspirational speaker and visual storyteller. A 2 times Canadian Provincial Award winner;

Leading Women Building Communities recognition program.

Volunteer recognition Multiple Sclerosis Society. 2015 crowned first female Ambassadorial Town Crier for Cobourg, Ontario Canada. An accomplished professional speaker and speech writer, Mandy is the recipient of the Prestigious Distinguished Toastmaster Award. Published professional poet, commissioned to create poems for events and ceremonies. Published Photographer. Women's Empowerment Coach.

I Am Blessed

Today I woke to the awareness that life coursed
through my veins.
My body moved as if on autopilot
To stretch the bones muscles and tendons.
The shrill call of squirrels scurrying outside my
window ... warmed my heart
I am blessed to be alive!
Another new day has dawned for me to make a
difference.
I am blessed
It is remembrance day ... many lives were lost to
give me my freedom
That I could thank them one by one
That I could hug until there is no more want
That I could express my pride and love
Do they know?
Can they feel my energy transmuting time space
and matter ?
I am blessed
Gratitude embraces every moving cell within
I see
I hear
I taste
I touch
I breathe in divinely imbued fragrances

I light the way by leading the way.

To know that those lost could feel cherished as I
cherish them always
Somehow ... I do know
I am blessed
New hope has dawned in my soul
Treasured precious moments brought to birth
Who needs a piece of my heart ?
Who cherishes my beautiful smile?
I heard just yesterday that when my name comes
into their mind ... a certain beloved soul sisters
face lights up..
"God I love you so much !"
I am blessed
For this is my purpose
To inspire and change lives
To raise the downtrodden and weary
To help them to find their light and shine as
brilliantly as the stars that they are!
You are worthy
You are deserving
You are loved
You are a blessing to this world
I touch their energy with passion
Blending as one ... they don't want to let go
I am blessed
Greatness exists in all
I love helping others to seek their greatness
To rise with renewed hope and joy
To become unstoppable in every endeavour

I light the way by leading the way.

I am blessed
Keep me humble great Father
For I have no need of praise
Your Divine gifts are my reward
Watching another change and grow
These are my rewards
I am blessed
I traverse my day looking for opportunities to
capture and preserve
To ponder over and become absorbed in
I see and hear what many do not.
Giving rise to new creative ideas
Open to all of life's magic unfolding in this
present moment in time.
I am blessed
I am blessed
I am grateful .
I ... am. .. grateful

I light the way by leading the way.

On Such A Day

Had hoped for a peaceful night
At 1 a.m .... at 3 a.m street noise broke the silence
Endless turmoil of screams and shouts
I desperately need sleep but attempts are to no avail.

At some unknown point in time
My eyes succumbed to lids heavy with fatigue
They stirred on a new day at 10 a.m
Awakened in life to begin yet again!

Slow and sluggish to rise and react
There'll be no haste or definition of movement
Muscles ache, joints grind, time will tell
Methodical stretching will uncoil the mechanism.

Even my loyal companion has not stirred
Stretched out on her right side deep in slumber
The drapes heave their clefts to the left and right
Day has long dawned, the sun is overhead!

I still ponder over the day before
A fundraiser for a 12 year old who could live no longer
Musicians, speakers, games and swag
A candlelit vigil, myself the orator capped it all.

Blessed with skills of communication and leadership
I reach out, passionately, to make a difference

I light the way by leading the way.

I hear truth, sincerity, honesty, I hear beauty
I see beauty in all that crosses my path
I believe in the good of everything.

Is that why my body rebels against my intentions?
Emotion and psychological involvement costs.
It takes your muscles, sinews, ligaments by storm
Hostage to the power beyond my control.

The day passes slowly..... meditatively
My pooch and I take life as it approaches
We are in no hurry, no expectations
Until intention wins, time to visit the world outside!

So my mantra spills from my thoughts
Get up! Dress up! And show up! To my life!
And that's exactly what I did
And such a day, became another, fantastic day!

I light the way by leading the way.

Another Life

One who's wisdom was as rich as a black pearl
Who's inspiration influenced and uplifted the soul.
Just a look at times, just a smile unfolding
Warmth and welcome beamed as a beacon from his
face.

"We cannot control others but we can control our
reactions," he would say
He would encourage us to " change the way we look
at things,"
And those things in turn would change, his life all
about perspective.

Do we give ourselves, our time, and energy without
looking for a reward?
Give, give, just keep giving and watch the universe
open it's abundance to you
His life was the reality, for the more he gave, the
more he received.

Doctor Wayne Dyer Leaves a fathomless legacy
It will be as it has always been, as if he never left
He's seen it all, he's done it all, he's blessed us all.

I light the way by leading the way.

Dear Friend

It's been a while dear friend, time knows no boundaries
We work, we play, we dance to the tune of life
Then with blunt force to our minds
We recall a moment of emptiness, dear friend I've missed you.

I dance, I write poetry, I speak in competition
I follow my dreams and passions to fruition
You raise a child, you run a business
You visit far away places with the love of your life.

Both of us strong, confident, independent women
Life and experience has polished the edges of our diamond personalities
A landscape before us depicts the great picture
In the big scheme of things, we ask ourselves; does it really matter?

The chord is tied between us, never to be undone
We know each other's thoughts, we have depth of understanding.
We reach that moment of emptiness together
One will call the other, who connects first in the race?

A treasured friendship has no material value
A treasured friendship lies within the fibres of the soul
A treasured friendship is never carrion for the birds of prey
Cast in stone, forged by the anvil, the hand of God brought us together, dear friend, we are blessed!

I light the way by leading the way.

Melancholy

The air fell heavy in the morning rain
The gloom and gray stillness took control
Wrapping the environment in its grip, like a vice
The more we struggle to escape, the tighter the
noose!

'Tis a hangman's life, searching for Victims to
beguile
We are not in mortal we are not free
Feel the knotted braid of tensile strength about your
throat
We breathe the same air, we escape not the same
eventuality.

Who stole the sunlight of penetrating rays?
Who decided it's time to cut short the days?
And stir a yearning for spring and new growth.
Of warmth seeping into pores and souls

'Twas the super moon this week with an eclipse!!
Late into the evening the clouds, dark clouds
gathered
Intent on veiling a once in a lifetime cosmic event
Intention turned to fruition as the lunar spectacle
disappeared from mortal sight.

I light the way by leading the way.

Days later and again late into the evening
A partial super moon hovered daringly, on a black
blanket
The universe allowing partial access to dynamic
energy
We pale in comparison to such grandiose
magnificence.

The canopy of darkness cloaked your face from the
light
Are you saddened by the fate of the night?
Is it a refuge from your solemn despair?
An oasis for your soul to lay it bare.

Still, dark waters plunge into fathomless depths
They lure, they catch and take you by the hand
The voice of an angel you ponder momentarily
Beware the camouflaged voice of the dead!!

Life remains hidden because of your forlorn demise
Can you shake the clouds, will you open your eyes?
This melancholy is fleeting oppression
Halt it's advance, summon retreat, take hold of
regression!

You defy my stature and freedom to behold the night
Who are you? How dare you trespass upon my soul!
Stand down!! With flight make your haste!
One life lost is more than enough, two or more, such
a terrible waste!

I light the way by leading the way.

Behold the courage, the strength and passion
Saving the life of another is no man's meagre ration
The spark arises amidst the burning embers of your
humanity
You are brave deserving of life, not drifting
throughout eternal strife.

The last vestiges of life's brutality
Have laid hold on me, like an orca tossing its prey
I can no more give my troth to life
The shroud is dark, yet clear, I am beckoned,
It's too, too late I'll tarry no more, I've had my day!

I light the way by leading the way.

Why?

Hearts are shackled
Shackle upon shackle

The human race burdened
Burdened with pangs of distress

Epic pandemic slaughter
Restraints to baring down, labour pains

No escape, liberty stolen
Revolution brews, fostering rebels

Wait, did we need to suffer yet more?
Murder, senseless, cruel, devastating

Tares the sinews from the flesh
Gouges love from the heart

Screams to the gods, WHY?
Screams fall on empty ears

Spattered blood, tepid taste in the mind
Heavy, exhausted, we are alone

We have no more strength
Our reserves are depleted

I light the way by leading the way.

Turmoil pervades the environment
The air is putrified with the stench of death

Fallen from grace, forlorn
How much more penance must we mete out?

Death knows no boundaries
Neither does life

Life prevails even after the dead are buried
Renews, lifts and exults

We are stronger than the iron forged from the bowels
of the earth
'Tis the storms that test our worth

You may have won on this day
You may have won at this time

But you have underestimated our resilience
Our determination to keep rising

Thunder, lightning, lashes of rain and ice,
Bellow from infinity if you must

This human fortress will not be trebuchet'd
We will stand and win, together fortified!!!

Esprit De La Mer

As the breeze gently ruffles tufts of grass
Crouched longingly beside a sauntering stream

As the light dances and plays games in between
the forest Giants

And the voices of the gods tickle your ears
carried along by the same haunting, lucid breeze

"Tis as timeless and ageless as the carved,
sculpted, chasm walls inside a vast Canyon

To have sensed and touched another's essence, is
like inhabiting a psycho physical awareness of
reaching deep inside your own soul

Where you are adorned, as a lover would
tenderly kiss and set on fire

All the yearnings of passion evoked unbridled
flames of desire

Great spirit of the ocean!

Goddess of infinity!

I light the way by leading the way.

To behold is to undo and peel back the layers of
words within the poet, that potentially may ne'er
pass this way again!

Effervescence Strikes The Lake

Silver serpent winds and weaves
Atop the satin disc of life
Overhead virgin cloud is tempted to settle.

The sun dances on a glass topped lake
The guardians of the shore protrude in stoic
formation
The host chorus applauds!

Planetary stalactite pierces infinity
Pervasive in all life forms.

Silver stalactite pierces the surface
Bronze hues erupt
We owe Him everything!!

I light the way by leading the way.

The Perfect Day

The perfect day, temperatures subdued from the
breath stealing humidity
A slight breeze moves leaves on trees into a
gentle dance mode
The sun tweaks between layers of foliage
Powder blue sky's hover above the backdrop on
the pallet of life below
Open top cars and vintage vehicles caress the
tarmac sauntering by
Small children lick their lips after the ecstasy of
ice cream, they grin excitedly
Humans are ready to throw care to the wind and
toss all feasible attire
The crowds are growing but will not reach
capacity for two more days
There are opportunities to saunter, observe, steal
pleasurable moments
A voice declares they went to the beach this
morning, another laughs, still another wonders
where the baby's shoes are.
A mother emphatically denies her Childs whim
" absolutely not!" she bellows
The cool air in the coffee shop tenderizes the
sights and sounds building around me.

I light the way by leading the way.

Did the building crowds observe the ants?
Is it in their DNA to swarm en masse and
behave haphazardly?
A poet, a poet laureate emeritus, a new poet
laureate in Tete a Tete collusion
To encourage and support an ancient transition
It is thee most perfect day!

I light the way by leading the way.

17

Hearken

Hearken unto the voice that tosses care to the wind

That softens the ache of the soul

That gives the unfathomable eternal gift...

I light the way by leading the way.

Just Observe

I sat and observed the winged insect
Whom yesterday I had swatted numerous times
Believing it was intent on stinging me

This day, as I let my mind wander
I felt only love for this tiny life.
It had a purpose too!
It lives on purpose.

It had located a hole in the wall, a haven of security
Its future offspring would be born within
Its Legacy would fly from here
Would find its own haven from which to begin again!

I felt peaceful and content, honoured that this
creature would teach me new learning.
I no longer desired to end its journey
I desire to watch and marvel at its knowing, its
intention, its purpose.

It would takeoff with power
It would return in a soft gentle landing
I know not of its destination
I could not detect its carrion upon return

Yet it returned again and again
And the more I observed, the more I revered
This tiny winged insect.

I light the way by leading the way.

Depth Unseen

My heart is open
Step into its depths
If you dare
I am far beyond what you can see
The priceless treasures are laid bare
For truth lies nestled deep within the heart of me!

I light the way by leading the way.

Cardinal Conversation

God's voice dips into my being
With His colourful sweet melodies
Through cardinal conversation in the tree top
And shrouded in the blazing rays of virgin sunlight.

I light the way by leading the way.

The Child In You, The Child In Me

The child in you, the child in me
Crouches up on the verge of expression,
So let's come from away as we take hold of this day
With joy and with fun as we run, dance and play!

Sheer abandonment and careless relent
We let go of tension and times not so well spent
To evoke the innocent curiosity that once burst into life
With sheer exuberance and happiness, we knew no strife!

We were excited for the rain to jump in a puddle
Or gather to share secrets we loved the huddle.

An old box became a countertop for let's play store!
Our friends eagerly wanted to come and explore.
Time new no boundaries as life was one big land of dreams
I can fly! I can dance! I can run like the wind!
Why look at me I'm the conductor of the band!

We sat in the grass and strung beads on strands
We told the globe on a desk
And imagined singing in far away lands.

Climbs trees, surmounting fences, running wild and free
No sense of time or dangers
Innocent bliss we could talk to strangers
Such was the child in you, and the child in me.

I light the way by leading the way.

Friends and girls alike to sit on the playground and play
Jax!
Or rollerskates to race down the street
Snowballs on sleighs on a crisp winters day
We care not if our hands and feet might freeze.

Laughter, squeals, gleeful and happy
Beneath the sun or a moonlit shadow
Nothing could touch the soul full of boundless energy
Cheeks a glow with rosy hues of effervescence.

Adults looked upon the child in you and the child in me
Noticing that life for us was all about play
No restrictions arms open wide
Awakened each day to the sheer thrill of the ride!

We learned to bake with flour on our faces
Polished and shined shoes that have neat looking laces
School uniforms made us blend into the crowd
You're growing up now young lady somethings are just not
allowed!

Yet today as we gather to recall
Step in to treasured memories where we had it all.

The dress up gowns that hung in staunch like closets
We did step in and bring them to light.
Exquisite diamontes that brought us a crowned delight
Why look at the lipstick and powder on the dressing table
Tiny hands with soon enabled!

Shoes so big that swallowed our feet whole
Smacked, and clipped the floor as we dragged them along
We loved playing queen, or bride, actress or dancer that
befit our role.

I light the way by leading the way.

Giggles and twirls canvases of imagination
We only knew how to make things up
Everything we touched came to life
Brought forth untamed spirits in unbridled fashion
We loved the power of our imagination!

We role-played, we cried with scraped up knees
We hugged 'neath the canopy of overhead trees.
Let's stay strong! Let's never grow up!
Let's hold his precious time of our lives
In the stardust, and the wind, in the pockets of our souls.

For who says the child in you and the child in me
Must be left behind to fade and die?

This child of divinity born
Has travelled through time
To arrive here today.
She never left you
She's here to stay!!

So rise up my diamond beauties
Emancipate your playful side
Today we dance!
Today we play!
From life itself we'll never hide!!

For ... I see the child in you
Please.....come play with the child in me!

Avalanche of Today - No mercy

Today I was taken by surprise
Storms had their relentless way with our shoreline on Lake
Ontario
Battering avalanches on the war path
To lay siege and never let go!

She came unannounced laden with swag
Heavy and iron like clad
She would take no prisoners all
Bound and swept in huge drifts
Visibility dissipated throughout the squall!

Slice and gust, sharp and savage
Exposed flesh might last a minute without shelter
Where can I run to where can I hide?
Piercing ice pellets amidst wind driven snow
You're mine I'll ne'er let go!

Tufts of frozen spray whip the cusp of a wave
That implodes under a rolling friend
For there is always another to take their place
The avalanche God will show no grace!

Vulgar deep purple almost black
Strikes the Caribbean emerald green waiting on the horizon
Bolt lightning hovers craftily behind the scene
Roaring wind and crashing wave
Human you are frail and feeble, destined to become my
slave!

I light the way by leading the way.

Treading where the elements have walked for aeons gone
by
You dare to defy the deities
Find the crevices and crawl inside
Alas we are porous, and our sweep is wide!

I stand before you in awe
Humbled by your magnificent power!
I know I am but of mortal flesh and bones
In this moment in time my life could end in a blustery
shower.

I hold my ground to absorb your energy
The wind whips and cuts into my face I feel a trickle.
I now believe and know beyond all shadow of a doubt
That you always take no prisoners
You refrain from extending the hand of grace to any mortal
soul.

For yours is the dynamic energy to hold sway over o'er
None can halt your path, disturb its course
To let go now is to gain eternal freedom
And so I become as one with the elements from which I
was crafted
Honoured and receptive, of blending with the Great Spirit!

I light the way by leading the way.

Baked

Awakened in a hot sweat, heavy air beating down my
lungs
Flailing arms attempt to disperse the mass to no avail
My body's core heats, my body's core heats taking no
prisoners

Blood cells errupt into frantic movement
We must cool the core, we must!
Water droplets attempt to fall from my skin eager to
assist the cool down
They evaporate into the mass, the mass, has no
intention of allowing life-saving aid!

I dream of cold icy water trickling into my mouth
permeating my soul
The sun beats down, my body bares down
The oasis is only off my mind
Oxygen has depleted
Alveoli pockets sag, empty of fortitude.

Consciousness is seeping away
There is no relief in sight
The mind hallucinates
The heart cannot withstand
Baked in the harshness of an arid, cold and empty
land....

I light the way by leading the way.

Echoes of The Heart

The heart echoes its reason to live
It will never quit!

As long as you beat within the chambers of my soul
You will live to love.
And you will know no other hollowed out crevice.

You will dance!
You will sing!
You will thrive!

Generations will fade in your wake
Your legacy will stand the storms of eternity

Just as the battered rain drenched canyons stand tall
to the stars

WE ..... NEVER .... QUIT!!

I light the way by leading the way.

The Tease

A slight chill in the air touches lips
A hint of what is to come, but still out of reach.
How's the green enveloped a hue of bronze?
All the leaves beginning to crinkle and fall?

Butterflies and birds have begun migration
Not much time now to plant and grow vegetables
Bales of hay stack up in fields now flattened
Blocks of bronze rising to touch the skyline.

The great ball of fire in the sky loses its hold
Gradually it's warmth is withdrawn further and
further
Clothing takes on a new look of protection
Jackets, sweaters, socks and pants become the norm.

But wait! On scantily clad days the air is warm
Such a tease of summer times before winter storms
Long flowing tendrils of warmth waft in a circle
You relax, and embody the tender warmth of now.

An evening haze, reflections and highlights
Of a late summers afternoon spilling over
Onto concrete roads and boulevards pleasant
underfoot
But time is of the essence, for soon frigid cold will
become a thief.

I light the way by leading the way.

And then, as if daring us to believe it was all a tease
Humidity returns, descending as a heavy canopy
The heat re-invades our souls and we are once more
parched
The sun beats hard, relentless leaving entrails of
fatigue.

If our existence was not already established here,
We could be made to believe in an eternal inferno!

Nature at its best dances to its own rhythms
It's not at our beck and call to be dominated
We are at the mercy of the tunes that it plays
Hot, cold, warm, chili, sun, rain, over these we have
no sway.

We are played with as a cat teases a mouse it has
caught
Nature allows us to feel some freedom, a moment to
pause, to believe
And as it tires of our feeble efforts it steps it up
No more the tease, we are subjected to reality!

I light the way by leading the way.

30

Trust

You need to go deep inside and ask
How do I let go? How do I trust?
I shouldn't need to know
Why is it so hard to let go?

There is nothing wrong everything is OK
As the universe conspires to forge an outcome
One that may not be my hearts desire
Yes one, that will be the right one, at the right time.

What do I love to do that stirs a revolution in my heart?
Don't stop, don't think, don't breathe, just go and do it!
Do it without hesitation.

Life always has a way of working out
And life always continues there's never a doubt
Made of the same elements of the planet we live upon
From aeons of time ago, beyond space, beyond the sun.

Our atmosphere pulsates from the depths of it's core
Thunderous applause pounds the open shore
Feelings are real too, not to be ignored
Acknowledge them, let them go then applaud.

Just trust, trust in goodness kindness and love
Of these qualities we can never soak up enough
You are loved, I am loved, we are one
No room for fears, doubts or worry, just trust and let them
be gone.

I light the way by leading the way.

Ancient Lamp

Egyptian papyrus reflected in your spiralled curve,
Adorned aloft life and death.

I can feel the heart beat in you that pulsates from the
ground of your birth
Saturating your ancient wooden base.

Your life permeates in the illumination of your
history oh ancient lamp
Where raw, unadulterated tones and hues
Would seep and infest both sap and bark alike.

When your light hails from the gloom
Darkness is shattered and dispelled,
Your brightness lays bare all that is and has ever
been.

As water permeates a rock face over time
Your brilliance leaves no crevice in which to hide.
Boldly erect, stately, staunch and heavy
You remain eternal, impregnable, evolving history
under your halo.

Oh ancient lamp tell me your stories
Beg me pay heed!
I will lay beneath you drenched and besotted,
enriched by your wisdom and vision
You the sage, and I the student.

I light the way by leading the way.

Allow Flow

Soothing balm, settle into it, oh my soul
No not the monotony of the mind
Step into waves that drift through silence
On into eternal bliss where the meaning of life
unfolds
His canvas where He sculpts and smooths the
gaping crevices
Touched lightly with tranquillity
Seeks solitude within the open chambers
Patience with softness spreads its canopy
There are no choices to be made
Devoid of decisions and mass abruption
Calm breaks the rhythms and patterns of the
depth where answers await!
Freedom clothes the scene I behold
There is no effort needed
There is only life, being, knowing
Each with its purpose no thought of necessity
A given moment in time passes, yet fulfilled
On to the next moment and it too passes
Colours of seasons spawn in the wake of time
Stillness clutches the fronds of subjection to the
wind, whispers to the leaves, lifts the lowly.
Into the great divide between that which is
physical and that which is immortal

I light the way by leading the way.

Oh beautiful maiden of the spirit
Your wings are strong your countenance Divine,
songbirds with voices that dance
Implore you hear their melodies
Hear them within your heart of hearts
Remain in love, the love from which you
emanate
For there is no other, and, you already know this,
you've already won the day!

All is well!!

I light the way by leading the way.